DEC

793
817
K

85-73

Keller, Charles

Grime Doesn't Pay.

DAT

GRIME DOESN'T PAY

GRIME DOESN'T PAY

LAW & ORDER JOKES

compiled by Charles Keller

illustrated by Jack Kent

Prentice-Hall, Inc., Englewood Cliffs, New Jersey

Printed in the United States of America •J

Prentice-Hall International, Inc., London
Prentice-Hall of Australia, Pty. Ltd., Sydney
Prentice-Hall Canada, Inc., Toronto
Prentice-Hall of India Private Ltd., New Delhi
Prentice-Hall of Japan, Inc., Tokyo
Prentice-Hall of Southeast Asia Pte. Ltd., Singapore
Whitehall Books Limited, Wellington, New Zealand
Editora Prentice-Hall do Brasil LTDA., Rio de Janeiro

10 9 8 7 6 5 4 3 2

Library of Congress Cataloging in Publication Data

Keller, Charles.
  Grime doesn't pay.

  Summary: A collection of jokes focusing on the law.
  1. Law—Anecdotes, facetiae, satire, etc.—Juvenile
literature. [1. Law—Wit and humor. 2. Jokes] 1. Title.
PN6231.L4K44 1984   818′.5402   83-22894
ISBN 0-13-365503-2

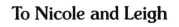

To Nicole and Leigh

What diploma do criminals get?
The third degree.

I hear the bank is looking for a teller.
I thought they hired one a month ago.
That's the one they're looking for.

What do you call a policeman's uniform?
A lawsuit.

We are accusing your son of starting the fire.
Our son?
Yes, arson.

My neighbor always whistles while he works.
He must be a happy guy.
No, he's a traffic cop.

I read that the FBI has one million fingerprints in
one room.
Really? I wish someone would tell my mother. I get
yelled at for the same thing.

The other night a robber pulled a knife on me, but
he wasn't a professional.
How do you know?
The knife still had butter on it.

Boy, that guy is really dumb. There was a sign in the post office that said, "Man wanted for robbery in New York."
So, what about it?
He applied for the job.

What would you do if a man with a shotgun demanded all your pickles?
Give him both barrels.

My mother heard a scary noise last night. She
jumped out of bed and saw a pair of feet sticking
out from under the bed.
Was it a burglar?
No, it was my father. He heard the noise, too.

Did you hear about the dumb guy who was
counterfeiting dollar bills?
No, what about him?
He was rubbing the zeros off tens.

Why didn't you stop when I blew my whistle?
I'm a little deaf.
**Don't worry. Here's a court summons. You'll get
your hearing in the morning.**

**I know a guy who made a fortune in crooked
dough.**
You mean he's a counterfeiter?
No, a pretzel baker.

Who shoots people, blows them up, then lets them go home and hang themselves?
A photographer.

I'm sorry I took the car, your honor.
Why did you take it?
It was parked in front of a cemetery and I thought the owner was dead.

Why are you opening that safe with your bare feet?
It only takes a few minutes longer and it drives the fingerprint experts crazy.

Did the newspaper give a description of the missing bank teller?
Yes, he was five feet ten inches tall and about $50,000 short.

This is a stickup. Your money or your life.
You'd better take my life, I need my money for my old age.

You were driving seventy-five miles per hour!
That's impossible. I've only been driving for fifteen minutes.

The police are coming! Quick, jump out the window!
But we're on the thirteenth floor!
This is no time to be superstitious.

Why did the robber take a bath?
He wanted to make a clean getaway.

Why are you in prison?
I was driving a car too slowly.
You mean too fast, don't you?
No, too slowly. The police caught up with me.

The police are looking for a man with one leg named Smith.
Oh? What's his other leg called?

I just finished a long run on Broadway.
What was the name of the play?
What play? A mugger chased me ten blocks.

Did you hear about the person who died by the open manhole?
They called it sewer-cide.

What kind of robbery is not dangerous?
A safe robbery.

It took me three months to finish my last book.
So what? It took me five years to finish my last
sentence.

**How can you be sure you were only going fifteen
miles per hour?**
Because I was going to the dentist.

**What do you get when you cross a police dog with
a skunk?**
Law and odor.

Why did the outlaw carry a bottle of glue when he went to rob the train?
He wanted to stick up the passengers.

If there was a kidnapping, what would you do?
Wake him up.

What happened when the prisoners put on a play?
It was a cell-out.

A robber who just got out of jail is looking for a job. What kind of work is he looking for?
Oh, he'll take anything.

Why was the farmer arrested in the morning?
Because he hit the hay the night before.

What happens when the police take a burglar's fingerprints?
It creates a bad impression.

What's the difference between a jeweler and a jailor?
A jeweler sells watches; a jailor watches cells.

Why did the prisoners in jail want to catch the measles?
So they could break out.

What makes potatoes good detectives?
They keep their eyes peeled.

That burglar tried to tell the police he was the invisible man.
Really?
Yes, but the police saw right through him.

What happened when the police caught the hot dog?
They grilled it.

Did you hear the joke about the body-snatcher?
No.
I won't tell you—you might get carried away.

What happens to a person who steals watches?
The lawyer gets the case, and the judge gives him time.

What kind of party do prisoners like best?
A going-away party.

Why was the skunk arrested for counterfeiting?
He was giving out bad scents.

What did the criminal say when he was saved from the hangman at the last minute?
"No noose is good noose."

Why did the spy spray his room with insect repellent?
He thought it was bugged.

Are you the defendant in this case?
No, not me.
Then who are you?
I'm the one who robbed the bank.

Did you hear about the holdup on the clothesline?
Two clothespins held up a pair of pants.

What's a frozen policeman?
A copsicle.

What kind of dog says "Meow"?
An undercover police dog.

There are hundreds of ways of making money but only one honest way.
What's that?
I knew you wouldn't know.

I know a guy who stole parts from ten different cars and put them all together.
What did he get?
Twenty years.

What do outlaws eat for dessert?
Crookies.

I'm afraid I've got to give you a ticket. That sign you passed said, "Speed limit—25 miles per hour."
But officer, how can I read those signs when I'm going sixty miles per hour?

What did the robber give his wife for her birthday?
A stole.

You are charged with committing over five hundred crimes in the last two years. What have you got to say for yourself?
Well, nobody's perfect.

Have you ever appeared in this court before?
Yes, your honor.
In what suit?
My dark blue one.

Why are you crossing the street when the sign says, "Don't walk"?
Oh, I thought it was an ad for a bus company.

You are a habitual criminal. Haven't you ever done anything for anyone else?
Well, I kept three or four detectives working regularly.

Can I help you, sir?
Yes, officer, did one of your men lose this ticket? I found it on my windshield.

What's a hangman's favorite reading material?
A noosepaper.

Hey, what are you doing up in my apple tree?
I saw a sign that said to keep off the grass.

Someone picked my pocket.
What did he get?
Practice.

Why were you driving so fast?
My brakes didn't work, and I was hurrying home
before I had an accident.

**When you saw that car coming toward you, why
didn't you give him half the road?**
I would have if I knew which half he wanted.

What did the judge do with that hit-and-run driver?
He sent him to the prison baseball team.

Why is a baker like a bank robber?
Because they always have their hands in dough.

My aunt is a kleptomaniac.
Is she taking anything for it?

Guilty or not guilty?
What else have you got?

I must charge you for murder.
All right. What do I owe you?

Tell me, officer, do you practice shooting your pistol into those little circles?
No, I'm a square shooter.

**As your attorney, I'm sorry I couldn't do more for
you.**
Thanks. Ten years is plenty.

**This is the tenth time you've been in court this year.
Aren't you ashamed to be seen in court so often?**
Why, no, your honor, I always thought it was a very
respectable place.

What is the prisoner's name?
81469.
Is that his real name?
No, that's only his pen name.

What driver never gets a ticket?
A screwdriver.

You are sentenced to 100 years in prison.
Your honor, I will never live long enough to finish that sentence.
Don't worry, just do the best you can.

The jury has found you innocent of stealing.
Does that mean I can keep the watch?

You can't park your car here.
Why not? The sign says, "Fine for parking."

What do you get when you cross a police dog with a mole?
An animal that brings law and order to the underground.

What does your uncle do for a living?
He's in the up-lift business.
Up-lift business?
Yes, he goes around saying, "Stick 'em up."

Ten days or $50.
I'll take the $50.

Judge, I can't be a forger. Why, I can't even sign my own name.
You are not accused of signing your own name.

What happened to the man who stole the calendar?
He got twelve months.

My wife has been throwing things at me ever since we got married.
Then why didn't you complain before?
This is the first time she hit me.

What does your brother do?
He's connected with the police department.
How?
By a pair of handcuffs.

Didn't you hear me whistling at you?
Sure, officer, but I don't flirt when I'm driving.

Today you are being released from jail. I hope you've learned your lesson.
I sure did. The next job I pull I'm wearing gloves.

You admit breaking into the same dress shop four times. What did you steal?
A dress for my wife. But she made me exchange it three times.

Do you swear to tell the truth, the whole truth, and nothing but the truth?
Why not? I'll try anything once.

Are you guilty or not guilty?
Not guilty.
Have you ever been in court before?
No, this is the first time I ever stole anything.

Why was the belt arrested?
For holding up the pants.

Why do watchdogs bark?
Because a robber wouldn't be frightened away by a meow.

A cement truck collided with a police van carrying prisoners.
What did the police do?
They're looking for ten hardened criminals.

Let's count the loot and see how much we made on this robbery.
I'm tired. Let's wait and look it up in the morning paper.

Excuse me, have you seen a policeman around here?
No, I haven't.
All right, then give me your money.

Have you any last words before you die in the electric chair?
Yes, I'd like to give my seat to a lady.

I haven't seen you for a while. Where have you been?
I've been away for thirty days.
Doing what?
Thirty days.

You are charged with running through an intersection and speeding.
Your honor, I was trying to get through it as fast as possible.

Which policemen play tennis?
Members of the racket squad.

In Los Angeles a man is hit by a car every five minutes.
Boy, I'll bet he's pretty beat up.

Did you know Jesse James was a weight-lifting champ?
Yes. He held up two ten-ton trains one after another.

We'll give you anything you want for your last meal.
Can I have champagne?
Sure, what year?
1998.

I saw a robber running down the street.
Did the police catch him?
No, he stepped on a scale and got a weigh.

Did you hear about the burglar alarm?
No, what about it?
The burglar didn't hear it either. That's why he's in jail.

Guilty or not guilty?
I don't know. I haven't heard the evidence yet.

Don't you know that crime doesn't pay?
Yes, but the hours are good.

My brother picks up things easily.
What kind of work does he do?
He's a shoplifter.

The police arrested an artist yesterday.
Did he confess?
No, he said he was framed.

Did you hear the joke about the murderer?
No, but I'll bet it's a killer.

Why did the dog go to court?
Because it got a barking ticket.

What happens when you illegally park a frog?
You get toad away.

Why do they call electric chairs period furniture?
Because they end a sentence.

What did the out-of-shape burglar risk when he was chased by the policeman?
Cardiac arrest.

I suppose you're going to tell me you weren't speeding.
I was speeding all right. But I was testing you to see if you were paying attention.

Did you hear about the wall that turned to a life of crime?
Yes, it went around holding up ceilings.

I had a watch stolen from under my nose last night.
Well, that's a funny place to wear it.

You are charged with driving eighty miles an hour in the middle of the night with no lights on.
I had to, your honor, the car was stolen.

What happened when the peanut got mugged?
It was assaulted.

My uncle came to this country knowing only two words in English and made a fortune.
What were the two words?
Hands up!

Somebody robbed the bakery yesterday.
Boy, that really takes the cake.

Put your hands down, this is a stick-up!
Don't you mean put your hands up?
Don't confuse me, this is my first job.

I hear your brother is in the holdup business.
Yes, he sells belts and suspenders.